MW01505481

Context:
Leader Guide

Context
Putting Scripture in Its Place

Context

978-1-7910-3209-8

978-1-7910-3210-4 *eBook*

Context: DVD

978-1-7910-3213-5

Context: Leader Guide

978-1-7910-3211-1

978-1-7910-3212-8 *eBook*

Also by Josh Scott:

Bible Stories for Grown-Ups

Josh Scott

PUTTING SCRIPTURE IN ITS PLACE

LEADER GUIDE

Abingdon Press | Nashville

Context:
Putting Scripture in Its Place
Leader Guide

Copyright © 2024 Abingdon Press
All rights reserved.

No part of this work may be reproduced or transmitted in any form or by any means, electronic or mechanical, including photocopying and recording, or by any information storage or retrieval system, except as may be expressly permitted by the 1976 Copyright Act, the 1998 Digital Millennium Copyright Act, or in writing from the publisher. Requests for permission can be addressed to Rights and Permissions, The United Methodist Publishing House, 810 12th Avenue South, Nashville, TN 37203-4704 or emailed to permissions@abingdonpress.com.

978-1-7910-3211-1

Scripture quotations unless noted otherwise are taken from the New Revised Standard Version, Updated Edition. Copyright © 2021 National Council of Churches of Christ in the United States of America. Used by permission. All rights reserved worldwide.

Scripture quotations noted CEB are taken from the Common English Bible. Copyright © 2011 by the Common English Bible. All rights reserved.

MANUFACTURED IN THE UNITED STATES OF AMERICA

CONTENTS

INTRODUCTION

An oft-quoted old saying in some preaching circles says, "Any text without context is a pretext." In *Context: Putting Scripture in Its Place,* Josh Scott, lead pastor of GracePointe Church in Nashville, Tennessee, encourages all Christians to take a second look (or third, or fourth, or even further look) at six Bible verses and stories widely "familiar" to Christians and even the wider culture in isolation—some of what Josh at one point calls the Bible's "Greatest Hits"—within their biblical context. When we do so, we may find these "familiar" texts aren't saying what we thought or were told they were saying. We can avoid using them as pretexts and "proof texts" for attitudes and actions that may align more with our culture than the Gospel and can instead hear them as God's living and challenging Word, summoning us to greater, more creative and loving, and more faithful discipleship.

This Leader Guide is designed to help small groups engage *Context* and the biblical passages it addresses. Its six sessions correspond to the chapters of Josh's book:

Session 1: A More Excellent Way (1 Corinthians 13)
Session 2: "Your People Will Be My People" (Ruth 1:16 CEB)
Session 3: "You Always Have the Poor with You" (Mark 14:7)
Session 4: "For Surely I Know the Plans I Have for You"
      (Jeremiah 29:11)

Session 5: "I Can Do All Things Through Him Who Strengthens Me"
(Philippians 4:13)
Session 6: Sodom and Gomorrah (Genesis 19)

Each session contains the following elements to draw from as you plan six in-person, virtual, or hybrid sessions:

+ Session Objectives
+ Biblical Foundations–Scripture texts for the session, in the New Revised Standard Version, Updated Edition or Common English Bible.
+ Before Your Session–Tips to help you prepare a productive session.
+ Starting Your Session–Discussion questions intended to "warm up" your group for fruitful discussion.
+ Book Discussion Questions–You likely will not be able or want to use all the questions in every session, so feel free to pick and choose based on your group's interests, leaving room for the Spirit to lead your discussion!
+ Closing Your Session–A focused discussion to help participants move from reflection in the session to planning action beyond it.
+ Opening and Closing Prayers

Thank you for leading your group in this study of *Context*. Leaders like you, committed to facilitating Christian education in congregations, help ensure that God's people continue to grow not only in their understanding of Scripture but also in their commitment to living out the values to which, through the Bible's ancient pages, God still calls us.

A More Excellent Way

(1 Corinthians 13)

SESSION OBJECTIVES

This session will help participants:

+ Think about the popularity of 1 Corinthians 13 in wedding ceremonies.

+ Appreciate 1 Corinthians as an actual letter Paul wrote to a specific congregation for practical, pastoral reasons.

+ Explore three core conflicts in the Corinthian congregation—over personalities, over abuse of the communal meal, and over spiritual gifts—as reflections of problematic hierarchies, and the ways Paul sought to guide the Corinthians through these conflicts.

+ Understand why Paul commended *agape* love as a "more excellent way" for the Corinthian congregation.

+ Identify ways their congregation currently expresses *agape* love, and how it could grow in expressing such love.

BIBLICAL FOUNDATIONS

If I speak in the tongues of humans and of angels but do not have love, I am a noisy gong or a clanging cymbal. And if I have prophetic powers and understand all mysteries and all knowledge and if I have all faith so as to remove mountains but do not have love, I am nothing. If I give away all my possessions and if I hand over my body so that I may boast but do not have love, I gain nothing.

Love is patient; love is kind; love is not envious or boastful or arrogant or rude. It does not insist on its own way; it is not irritable; it keeps no record of wrongs; it does not rejoice in wrongdoing but rejoices in the truth. It bears all things, believes all things, hopes all things, endures all things.

Love never ends. But as for prophecies, they will come to an end; as for tongues, they will cease; as for knowledge, it will come to an end. For we know only in part, and we prophesy only in part, but when the complete comes, the partial will come to an end. When I was a child, I spoke like a child, I thought like a child, I reasoned like a child. When I became an adult, I put an end to childish ways. For now we see only a reflection, as in a mirror, but then we will see face to face. Now I know only in part; then I will know fully, even as I have been fully known. And now faith, hope, and love remain, these three, and the greatest of these is love.

(1 Corinthians 13:1-13)

Now I appeal to you, brothers and sisters, by the name of our Lord Jesus Christ, that all of you be in agreement and that there be no divisions among you but that you be knit together in the same mind and the same purpose. For it has been made clear to me by Chloe's people that there are quarrels among you, my brothers and sisters. What I mean is that each of you says, "I belong to Paul," or "I belong to Apollos," or "I belong to Cephas," or "I belong to Christ." Has Christ been divided? Was Paul crucified for you? Or were you baptized in the name of Paul?

(1 Corinthians 1:10-13)

Now in the following instructions I do not commend you, because when you come together it is not for the better but for the worse. For, to begin with, when you come together as a church, I hear that there are divisions among you, and to some extent I believe it. Indeed, there have to be factions among you, for only so will it become clear who among you are genuine. When you come together, it is not really to eat the Lord's supper. For when the time comes to eat, each of you proceeds to eat your own supper, and one goes hungry and another becomes drunk. What! Do you not have households to eat and drink in? Or do you show contempt for the church of God and humiliate those who have nothing? What should I say to you? Should I commend you? In this matter I do not commend you!...

Whoever, therefore, eats the bread or drinks the cup of the Lord in an unworthy manner will be answerable for the body and blood of the Lord. Examine yourselves, and only then eat of the bread and drink of the cup. For all who eat and drink without discerning the body eat and drink judgment against themselves. For this reason many of you are weak and ill, and some have died....

So then, my brothers and sisters, when you come together to eat, wait for one another.

(1 Corinthians 11:17-22, 27-30, 33)

Now there are varieties of gifts but the same Spirit, and there are varieties of services but the same Lord, and there are varieties of activities, but it is the same God who activates all of them in everyone. To each is given the manifestation of the Spirit for the common good. To one is given through the Spirit the utterance of wisdom and to another the utterance of knowledge according to the same Spirit, to another faith by the same Spirit, to another gifts of healing by the one Spirit, to another the working of powerful deeds, to another prophecy, to another the discernment of spirits, to another various kinds of tongues, to another the interpretation of tongues. All these are activated by one and the same Spirit, who allots to each one individually just as the Spirit chooses....

Now you are the body of Christ and individually members of it. And God has appointed in the church first apostles, second prophets, third teachers, then deeds of power, then gifts of healing, forms of assistance, forms of leadership, various kinds of tongues. Are all apostles? Are all prophets? Are all teachers? Do all work powerful deeds? Do all possess gifts of healing? Do all speak in tongues? Do all interpret? But strive for the greater gifts. And I will show you a still more excellent way.

(1 Corinthians 12:4-11, 27-31)

BEFORE YOUR SESSION

+ Carefully and prayerfully read this session's Biblical Foundations, more than once; if your preparation time allows, read 1 Corinthians in its entirety. Consult a trusted study Bible and/or commentaries for additional background information.

+ Carefully read *Context: Putting Scripture in Its Place*, chapter 1. Note topics about which you have questions or want to research further before your session.

+ You will need: Bibles for in-person participants and/or screen slides prepared with Scripture texts for sharing (note the translation you use); newsprint or a markerboard and markers (for in-person sessions).

+ If using the DVD or streaming video, preview the session 1 video segment. Choose the best time in your session plan for viewing it.

+ Prepare a handout and/or screen slide with the text of 1 Corinthians 13:4-7 for participants to read together in unison (see "Closing Your Session").

STARTING YOUR SESSION

Welcome participants. Tell them why you are excited about leading this study of *Context* by Josh Scott. Invite volunteers to speak briefly about why they are interested in this study and what they hope to gain from it.

Ask participants to think about either the most recent wedding or the most memorable wedding—other than their own, if they are married—they have attended. Ask:

+ What did you appreciate most about that wedding ceremony?
+ Was 1 Corinthians 13 read and/or talked about as part of the ceremony? If not, what readings, if any, were included?

+ If you are or have been married, do you remember what Scriptures, if any, were part of your wedding ceremony?

+ Why do you think 1 Corinthians 13 is a popular text for use in weddings?

Read aloud from *Context*: "Paul was not writing wedding liturgy when he wrote 1 Corinthians 13." Tell participants this session's study of these familiar words in their biblical context will help your group understand the apostle Paul's intent in writing them and what they might mean for Christians—married or unmarried—today.

OPENING PRAYER

God, as we engage these ancient words that were originally someone else's mail, we ask for wisdom to discern what they meant then and what they might mean now, for us. Help us hear them as if for the first time, and may we embrace their challenge for the way we relate to one another. Amen.

WATCH SESSION VIDEO

Watch the session 1 video segment together. Discuss:

+ What did Josh say in this video that most interested, intrigued, surprised, or confused you? Why?

+ What questions does this video raise for you?

BOOK DISCUSSION QUESTIONS

Somebody Else's Mail

Ask volunteers to talk about a time they read someone else's mail—whether by accident, at the intended recipient's request, or other circumstances. How did knowing they were not the person for whom the mail was meant affect their reading of it?

Have participants turn in their Bibles to 1 Corinthians. Recruit a volunteer to read aloud 1:1-9. Discuss:

+ How is the salutation (the greeting) of this letter like and unlike greetings in letters today?

+ What do you know and what can you infer about Paul from this greeting? about the Christian congregation in Corinth? about God and Christ?

+ Based on these verses, what are some topics you anticipate this letter might address?

+ How does remembering Paul wasn't intending to write, nor were his letters' recipients expecting to hear, sacred Scripture or systematic theology affect your understanding of his letters?

+ Josh points out that neither Paul nor any biblical author wrote "small chunks" meant to stand on their own. Short of reading entire biblical books at a time *every* time we read a given passage of Scripture, how should we take this fact into account in our Bible studies?

+ "Paul's letters are not instructions to individuals about what to believe, but to communities about how to behave toward one another." Do you think keeping this perspective in mind, as Josh encourages us to, makes Paul's letters more or less accessible to Christians today? more or less relevant? Why?

Paul and the Corinthians

Recruit a volunteer to read aloud 1 Corinthians 4:14-21. Discuss:

+ Describe Paul's attitude(s) toward the Corinthians in these verses.

+ On what basis does Paul distinguish between the Corinthians' many possible "mentors in Christ" (CEB; "guardians," NRSVue) and himself as their "father"? What is the significance of the parental metaphor Paul uses here?

Conflicts in Corinth

Form three groups of participants. Assign each group responsibility for reading and discussing one of these Biblical Foundations (including the verses in parentheses, as time permits, for additional context):

+ 1 Corinthians 1:10-13 (14-17)
+ 1 Corinthians 11:17-22, (23-26) 27-30, (31-32) 33(-34)
+ 1 Corinthians 12:4-11, (12-26) 27-31

Write these questions on markerboard or newsprint (and/or prepare them on a slide) for groups to refer to during their discussions:

+ What practical, pastoral conflict is Paul addressing in this passage?
+ How does the conflict threaten or harm the Corinthian congregation?
+ What theological questions or issues does the conflict raise?
+ How does Paul try to help the Corinthians move through the conflict?

Allow groups sufficient time for reading and conversation. ("Sufficient time" will vary based on session length and participant's previous Bible study experience, but try to allow at least 15 minutes.) When discussion time is over, invite a volunteer from each group to report highlights from their small group's discussion to the whole group.

Discuss the conflicts in Corinth further using some or all of these questions:

- ✦ How does the problem of hierarchy—which Josh says is the central problem Paul addresses in this letter—play a role in each of these Corinthian conflicts?
- ✦ How do each of these conflicts echo the disciples' argument at the Last Supper in Luke 22:24-27?
- ✦ How have you seen "celebrity culture" cause problems in churches, as it did in Corinth? What, specifically, can faith communities do to discourage it?
- ✦ How much or little does your congregation reflect the economic diversity of the Corinthian congregation? Why? How can congregations acknowledge and address economic *differences* among members without drawing hierarchical economic *distinctions?*
- ✦ When does your congregation eat together? To what extent are your congregational meals "a practical matter of doing justice"?
- ✦ How does your congregation help people discover and exercise their spiritual gifts? Do you recognize the spiritual gifts Paul mentions in members of your faith community? What other things, which Paul does not mention, do you consider spiritual gifts, and why?
- ✦ Is hierarchy an unavoidable part of Christian community? Why or why not? What formal or informal but no less real hierarchies exist in your congregation? Do they conflict with the "radically inclusive egalitarianism" Paul says defines the church in Galatians 3:28?

Alternative: If time or group size don't permit three smaller group discussions, discuss each conflict in Corinth briefly, or choose one to discuss in more depth.

The "More Excellent Way"

Recruit a volunteer to read aloud 1 Corinthians 13. Discuss:

+ Why does Paul call *agape* love a "more excellent way" (1 Corinthians 12:31) for the Corinthians?
+ Which of *agape* love's attributes, as Paul describes them, most comforts you? encourages you? challenges you?
+ How does hearing 1 Corinthians 13 in the context of the Corinthians' conflicts shape or reshape your understanding and appreciation of these words?

CLOSING YOUR SESSION

Josh recalls a youth group activity in which people read 1 Corinthians 13 aloud, replacing the word "love" with their own names. Invite participants to read 1 Corinthians 13:4-7 aloud together, replacing the word "love" with your congregation's name.

Invite responses to this question from *Context*: "If we were to overlay Paul's description of *agape* love onto our communities, where would we find congruence? Can we also imagine where we might have work to do?"

Before dismissing participants, encourage them to read the Book of Ruth before the next session.

CLOSING PRAYER

God, we long to cultivate the kind of equitable and generous community that Paul believed was possible. Guide us to resist the hierarchies that seek to divide and diminish the unity and togetherness that reflect the transformative love of God for everyone and everything. We are grateful to be in community, and we long for our life together to reflect the radical vision of the first Jesus communities. Amen.

SESSION 2

"Your People Will Be My People"
(Ruth 1:16 CEB)

SESSION OBJECTIVES

This session will help participants:

* Familiarize or re-familiarize themselves with the story of Ruth, making connections between this story of family surprises with such stories from their own families.

* Define and understand the key biblical concept of *hesed* and how it is an attribute of not only God but also Ruth.

* Evaluate Ruth as a possible response to the postexilic actions taken by Ezra in the sixth century BCE against intermarriages in Judah.

* Ponder how God has used outsiders and newcomers to create surprising possibilities for their community of faith.

BIBLICAL FOUNDATIONS

No Ammonite or Moabite shall come into the assembly of the Lord *even to the tenth generation. None of their descendants shall come into the assembly of the* Lord *forever.*

(Deuteronomy 23:3)

During the days when the judges ruled, there was a famine in the land. A man with his wife and two sons went from Bethlehem of Judah to dwell in the territory of Moab. The name of that man was Elimelech, the name of his wife was Naomi, and the names of his two sons were Mahlon and Chilion. They were Ephrathites from Bethlehem in Judah. They entered the territory of Moab and settled there.

But Elimelech, Naomi's husband, died. Then only she was left, along with her two sons. They took wives for themselves, Moabite women; the name of the first was Orpah and the name of the second was Ruth. And they lived there for about ten years.

But both of the sons, Mahlon and Chilion, also died. Only the woman was left, without her two children and without her husband.

Then she arose along with her daughters-in-law to return from the field of Moab, because while in the territory of Moab she had heard that the Lord *had paid attention to his people by providing food for them. She left the place where she had been, and her two daughters-in-law went with her. They went along the road to return to the land of Judah.*

Naomi said to her daughters-in-law, "Go, turn back, each of you to the household of your mother. May the Lord *deal faithfully with you, just as you have done with the dead and with me. May the* Lord *provide for you so that you may find security, each woman in the household of her husband." Then she kissed them, and they lifted up their voices and wept.*

But they replied to her, "No, instead we will return with you, to your people."

Naomi replied, "Turn back, my daughters. Why would you go with me? Will there again be sons in my womb, that they would be husbands for you? Turn back, my daughters. Go. I am too old for a husband. If I were to say that I have hope, even if I had a husband tonight, and even more, if I were to bear sons—would you wait until they grew up? Would you refrain from having a husband? No, my daughters. This is more bitter for me than for you, since the LORD's will has come out against me."

Then they lifted up their voices and wept again. Orpah kissed her mother-in-law, but Ruth stayed with her. Naomi said, "Look, your sister-in-law is returning to her people and to her gods. Turn back after your sister-in-law."

But Ruth replied, "Don't urge me to abandon you, to turn back from following after you. Wherever you go, I will go; and wherever you stay, I will stay. Your people will be my people, and your God will be my God. Wherever you die, I will die, and there I will be buried. May the LORD do this to me and more so if even death separates me from you."

(Ruth 1:1-17 CEB)

After these things had been done, the officials approached me and said, "The people of Israel, the priests, and the Levites have not separated themselves from the peoples of the lands with their abominations, from the Canaanites, the Hittites, the Perizzites, the Jebusites, the Ammonites, the Moabites, the Egyptians, and the Amorites. For they have taken some of their daughters as wives for themselves and for their sons. Thus the holy seed has mixed itself with the peoples of the lands, and in this faithlessness the officials and leaders have led the way." . . .

Then Ezra the priest stood up and said to them, "You have trespassed and married foreign women and so increased the guilt of Israel. Now make confession to the LORD the God of your ancestors and do his will; separate yourselves from the peoples of the land and from the foreign wives."

(Ezra 9:1-2; 10:10-11)

BEFORE YOUR SESSION

+ Carefully and prayerfully read the Book of Ruth (preferably more than once). Consult a trusted study Bible and/or commentaries for additional background information.

+ Carefully read *Context: Putting Scripture in Its Place*, chapter 2. Note topics about which you have questions or want to research further before your session.

+ You will need: Bibles for in-person participants and/or screen slides prepared with Scripture texts for sharing (note the translation you use); newsprint or a markerboard and markers (for in-person sessions).
+ If using the DVD or streaming video, preview the session 2 video segment. Choose the best time in your session plan for viewing it.

STARTING YOUR SESSION

Welcome participants. Invite them to think about their family histories and answer some or all of these questions:

+ Did your family migrate from one country to another? When? For what reasons? What stories does your family still tell about the journey?
+ What are the hardest circumstances your family has faced in its history? How did your family cope with them?
+ Have "outsiders" ever entered and become part of your family? What happened?
+ Who is the most surprising person to whom your family is related?

Tell participants this session explores a surprising family story from ancient Israel: the Book of Ruth, "someone who embraced another in a time of disaster and displayed great courage in the face of uncertainty."

OPENING PRAYER

God, your love extends beyond the lines and boundaries we have created. Open our eyes to see your faithful love for every person and open our hands and hearts to share it generously with others. Amen.

WATCH SESSION VIDEO

Watch the session 2 video segment together. Discuss:

+ What did Josh say in this video that most interested, intrigued, surprised, or confused you? Why?
+ What questions does this video raise for you?

BOOK DISCUSSION QUESTIONS

Moving to Moab

Recruit three volunteers to read aloud Ruth 1:1-17, taking the roles of the narrator, Naomi, Orpah (who speaks together with Ruth in verse 10), and Ruth. Discuss:

+ Why might Moab be a surprising destination for Elimelech, Naomi, and their sons? (See Deuteronomy 23:3.) What do you imagine this family might have felt about moving to Moab?
+ What crisis do Naomi and her daughters-in-law face about a decade later? What does Naomi decide to do? Why?
+ Why does Naomi urge Orpah and Ruth to stay in Moab? Why do you think they both initially want to go with her to Judah? Why do you think Orpah ultimately turns back?
+ Read Deuteronomy 25:5-10. What was levirate marriage? What social purposes did it serve? Why is it relevant to the situation in which Naomi, Orpah, and Ruth find themselves?
+ "Ruth, in her declaration of fidelity to Naomi, embraces Naomi's God, people, and land in an act of voluntary commitment." What do you think accounts for Ruth's commitment?
+ Josh says Ruth embodies *hesed*—a "covenant loyalty," a "faithful love," a "love and benevolence that are extended without any obligation." When have you seen or experienced such love between people?

- Josh points out Scripture repeatedly attributes *hesed* to God (Psalm 118:1; Exodus 34:6-7a). What Bible stories would you point to as examples or illustrations of God's *hesed?*
- What new name does Naomi take when she and Ruth reach Bethlehem, and why (1:19-21)? When, if ever, have you felt as she feels? Can her lament be a model of faithfulness for people today? If so, how so? If not, why not?
- Why does the narrator repeatedly remind readers that Ruth is a Moabite (1:22; 2:6)?

Hesed *Comes Full Circle*

Guide participants through a "highlights tour" of the rest of Ruth, using the passages cited below and the questions as a guide, as well as Josh's summary of it in *Context.*

Ruth 2:1-20

- What are your impressions of Boaz?
- Boaz followed the practice commanded in Leviticus 19:9-10. How does this commandment ensure "generosity and consideration"? How much do your society's laws "build in" generosity and consideration?
- Why does Boaz treat Ruth with kindness? Why does his kindness surprise her? What similar examples of unexpected kindness do you know of or have you experienced?
- How often, in your experience, does word of someone else's kindness (*hesed*) inspire kindness in others? When has it inspired kindness in you?
- Boaz makes it possible for Ruth to glean grain in abundance (2:15-17). When has someone shown you abundant generosity?
- How do Ruth's initiative, Boaz's generosity, and God's *hesed* (2:20) work together in this story for good?

RUTH 3:1-14

- How does Ruth both follow and diverge from Naomi's plan? Why does Ruth approach Boaz when she does? What do these actions show us about her?

- Boaz is a potential "next-of-kin" (3:9, 13) for Ruth and Naomi, as Josh explains, one who can provide protection for vulnerable relatives. Have you ever protected a vulnerable relative? Has a family member ever provided such protection and provision for you that you think of that person as a "redeemer"? What happened?

- How do you react to the sexual undertones (or, perhaps, overtones) in this story? What might they suggest about how God can use human sexuality for redemptive purposes?

- What obstacle still stands in the way of, as Josh says, the "happily ever after" in this story (3:12-13)?

RUTH 4:1-6

- Why does the closer next-of-kin refuse his right to redeem Elimelech's field? How much or how little do you think Boaz influences the next-of-kin's decision? Why?

- What's your opinion, if any, of this almost-redeemer kinsman? When, if ever, have you decided not to do something you otherwise might have done out of concern or fear for how it would affect your position? Would you make the same decision again? Why or why not?

RUTH 4:13-17

- How are human and divine activity again linked in this story's "happily ever after"?

+ Why do the women of Bethlehem tell Naomi that Ruth "is more to [her] than seven sons" (4:15)? Why do they say Obed "has been born to Naomi" (4:17)?
+ Who is Obed's famous grandson?

THE WHEN OF RUTH

Discuss:

+ When in biblical history is the story of Ruth set (1:1)? How does the book's placement in Christian Bibles reflect this setting? How do Ruth's choices and behavior contrast with the situation described in Judges 21:25 (see also Judges 17:6; 18:1; 19:1)?
+ In the Hebrew Bible (or TANAKH), the Book of Ruth is among the Writings, as are the books of Ezra and Nehemiah, which date from the people's return to Judah circa 538 BCE, after the Babylonian Exile. Why was the people's concern about their identity high during the time of return from exile?
+ Read Ezra 9:1-2; 10:10-11. Why do Ezra and the officials view the Israelites' marriages to women of other nations as a problem? What solution does Ezra command? What do you think and feel about Ezra's plan? Why?
+ If, as Josh argues, Ruth was written during the time of and even as a response to Ezra's reforms, how does this historical context shape the way you read and understand Ruth?
+ We have no biblical evidence that Ezra heard or read the Book of Ruth, but how do you imagine he would have responded if he had? Why?
+ "Isn't it a little surprising," asks Josh, "that both Ruth and Ezra-Nehemiah are in the canon of Scripture and even, within the

Hebrew Bible, in the same section?" Why do you think those who preserved and collected the sacred writings included these writings together?

+ When is concern for the identity and integrity of God's people a healthy and constructive concern? When and how can it become dangerous and unfaithful?

+ Does your congregation maintain its sense of identity without separating itself, intentionally or not, from certain kinds of people? How?

CLOSING YOUR SESSION

In *Context*, Josh concludes that Ruth's *hesed* created surprising new possibilities for God's people, and that she still invites us "to make space for surprises" rather than making decisions out of fear. Ask participants to think about either a time someone new to or outside of the congregation created a surprising new possibility for it; and/or a time the congregation made an important decision out of hope and trust, rather than fear. Ask: "What lesson(s) did our congregation learn that can help us face the future in greater faithfulness to God?"

CLOSING PRAYER

God, thank you for your faithful love. Help us to embody this kind of love to others, and to receive the same. We want to make space for surprises and to reject the fear that drives us apart. Amen.

SESSION 3

"You Always Have the Poor with You"

(Mark 14:7)

SESSION OBJECTIVES

This session will help participants:

+ Assess ways in which their relationship to and feelings about the Bible may have changed over time.

+ Articulate the significance of a woman's anointing of Jesus at Bethany, on its own terms and as the middle of a "story sandwich" in Mark 14:1-11.

+ Explore the "Sabbatical Year" commandment in Deuteronomy 15 as both the context for Jesus's comment about "the poor" and a biblical example of justice.

+ Distinguish between charity and justice and consider how much attention they and their congregations pay to each.

BIBLICAL FOUNDATIONS

It was two days before the Passover and the Festival of Unleavened Bread. The chief priests and the scribes were looking for a way to arrest Jesus by stealth and kill him, for they said, "Not during the festival, or there may be a riot among the people."

While he was at Bethany in the house of Simon the leper, as he sat at the table, a woman came with an alabaster jar of very costly ointment of nard, and she broke open the jar and poured the ointment on his head. But some were there who said to one another in anger, "Why was the ointment wasted in this way? For this ointment could have been sold for more than three hundred denarii and the money given to the poor." And they scolded her. But Jesus said, "Let her alone; why do you trouble her? She has performed a good service for me. For you always have the poor with you, and you can show kindness to them whenever you wish, but you will not always have me. She has done what she could; she has anointed my body beforehand for its burial. Truly I tell you, wherever the good news is proclaimed in the whole world, what she has done will be told in remembrance of her."

Then Judas Iscariot, who was one of the twelve, went to the chief priests in order to betray him to them. When they heard it, they were greatly pleased and promised to give him money. So he began to look for an opportunity to betray him.

(Mark 14:1-11)

"Every seventh year you shall grant a remission of debts. And this is the manner of the remission: every creditor shall remit the claim that is held against a neighbor, not exacting it, because the LORD's remission has been proclaimed. Of a foreigner you may exact it, but you must remit your claim on whatever any member of your community owes you. There will, however, be no one in need among you, because the LORD is sure to bless you in the land that the LORD your God is giving you as a possession to occupy, if only you will obey the LORD your God by diligently observing this entire commandment that I command you today. When the LORD your God has

blessed you, as he promised you, you will lend to many nations, but you will not borrow; you will rule over many nations, but they will not rule over you.

"If there is among you anyone in need, a member of your community in any of your towns within the land that the LORD *your God is giving you, do not be hard-hearted or tight-fisted toward your needy neighbor. You should rather open your hand, willingly lending enough to meet the need, whatever it may be. Be careful that you do not entertain a mean thought, thinking, 'The seventh year, the year of remission, is near,' and therefore view your needy neighbor with hostility and give nothing; your neighbor might cry to the* LORD *against you, and you would incur guilt. Give liberally and be ungrudging when you do so, for on this account the* LORD *your God will bless you in all your work and in all that you undertake. Since there will never cease to be some in need on the earth, I therefore command you, 'Open your hand to the poor and needy neighbor in your land.'"*

(Deuteronomy 15:1-11)

BEFORE YOUR SESSION

+ Carefully and prayerfully read Mark 14:1-11, several times. Consult a trusted study Bible and/or commentaries for additional background information.

+ Carefully read *Context: Putting Scripture in Its Place*, chapter 3. Note topics about which you have questions or want to research further before your session.

+ You will need: Bibles for in-person participants and/or screen slides prepared with Scripture texts for sharing (note the translation you use); newsprint or a markerboard and markers (for in-person sessions).

+ If using the DVD or streaming video, preview the session 3 video segment. Choose the best time in your session plan for viewing it.

STARTING YOUR SESSION

Welcome participants. Invite volunteers to talk briefly about some way in which their understanding of a Bible passage has changed as they have grown older. Be ready to talk briefly about such a shift from your own experience. Ask participants if they can say, along with Josh, that they have "[fallen] in love with the Bible," and why or why not. Assure participants their answer does not have to be "yes!" Faithful Christians can and do feel a wide range of things about the Bible even as they keep engaging it thoughtfully.

Tell participants this session explores a Bible quotation about which Josh's understanding changed as he grew older and engaged Scripture more. Ask whether participants have heard the quotation, "You always have the poor with you" used, as Josh heard it used, to argue against helping people in poverty, or against efforts to end poverty. Explain that this session will help your group hear this quotation in its larger context in hopes of understanding it better.

OPENING PRAYER

God, you are passionate about justice. You call us to join you in creating a world that is just and equitable for all your children. May we be your collaborators in bringing a better world into being. Amen.

WATCH SESSION VIDEO

Watch the session 3 video segment together. Discuss:

+ What did Josh say in this video that most interested, intrigued, surprised, or confused you? Why?
+ What questions does this video raise for you?

BOOK DISCUSSION QUESTIONS

The Anointing at Bethany

Recruit volunteers to read aloud Mark 14:3-9 as the narrator, Jesus, and one or more disciples (verses 4-5). Discuss:

+ Locate Jerusalem and Bethany on a map of first-century Judea (find such a map in a study Bible or other reference work, or online). Josh says Jesus's decision to journey to Jerusalem for the Passover in what would be the last week of his earthly ministry was "strategic and very dangerous." How so?

+ Josh says Bethany was the place Jesus went to "regroup" in safety and among friends. Why did Jesus need such a place? (Skim Mark 11–13 for context.) Where is your "Bethany," the place you go when, as Josh says, your life's "temperature [rises] too high"?

+ Josh says dining in Simon the leper's home "was a very Jesus thing to do." What does he mean? (See, for example, Mark 1:40-45; 2:15-17.) What can other people know about you from the people with whom you regularly share meals?

+ What does the woman's pouring of costly perfume on Jesus's head symbolize? What "bold claim" does it make about who Jesus is? How is her performance of this act unusual?

+ Why, explicitly, do Jesus's disciples scold the woman? What might be some other, implicit reasons they scold her?

+ Why does Jesus defend the woman and her action? What promise regarding it and her does Jesus make?

+ What do you imagine the woman thought and felt before, during, and after this incident? How do you think she would react to the fact that we don't know her name? How do you react to it?

You Will Always Have the Poor

Recruit a volunteer to read aloud Deuteronomy 15:1-2, 7-11. Discuss:

+ What economic practice is commanded every seventh year (verses 1-2)? For what reason(s) does God command this practice?

+ How is this "Sabbatical Year" like and unlike the weekly Sabbath God commands Israel to observe (Exodus 20:8-11; Deuteronomy 5:12-15)? How is it like and unlike the year of Jubilee commanded in Leviticus 25?

+ What potential for abusing this practice does the commandment explicitly address (verses 8-9)? Why?

+ How and why does this commandment assume a situation of abundance rather than scarcity among God's people? How does or ought this assumption inform the way God's people think about and use material resources today?

+ At the same time the commandment assumes abundance, it recognizes some people will always be in need (verse 11). Does the commandment contradict itself? Why or why not?

+ How does reading Jesus's words from Mark 14 in their original context in Deuteronomy 15 refute the idea that God and Jesus are decreeing poverty should always exist?

The Outside of the Sandwich

Recruit one volunteer to read aloud Mark 14:1-2 and another to read aloud 14:10-11. Explain, as Josh does, that Mark frequently uses a literary technique called "intercalation"—illuminating one story by framing or "sandwiching" it between two others. Discuss:

+ What is the main focus of the narrative frame in which Mark puts the story of the woman who anoints Jesus?

+ Josh points out Jesus's opponents were among the Temple leaders of Jesus's day. Jewish people, then or now, do not bear blame for Jesus's death. How have Christian misunderstandings and misinterpretations of the "inter-family disagreement" between Jesus and Temple leaders contributed to anti-Semitism and anti-Judaism throughout history? What are you and your congregation doing to reject anti-Jewish prejudice and hatred?

+ Why did Jesus critique the Temple's leaders (see 11:15-18)? Where would Jesus's critique of religious institutions and their leaders find targets today?

+ Why do you think Judas Iscariot chooses the moment he does to arrange his betrayal of Jesus? How do the "glaring contradictions" between Judas and the woman who anoints Jesus add to your understanding of the woman's actions?

Charity, Justice, and Imagination

+ What is the distinction between charity and justice? How, if at all, are the two connected? Is one more desirable than the other? Why or why not?

+ Do you agree with Josh that the "Sabbatical Year" commandment in Deuteronomy 15 is an example of justice rather than charity? Why or why not?

+ Do you agree with Josh that Jesus is, in Mark 14:7, calling his disciples to show the "kindness" of justice rather than charity to those who are poor? Why or why not?

+ Do you give more attention to charity or to justice in the way you spend your time and resources? Why?

+ Does your congregation?

- What are some of the root causes of poverty in today's society? What are you and your congregation doing—or what could you be doing—to address them as followers of Jesus?

- "We can sum up the failures of the disciples throughout Mark's narrative," Josh states, "as a *failure of imagination*." What specific obstacles prevented the disciples from successfully imagining the world Jesus came to proclaim and create? Why does Josh point to Judas as "the ultimate example" of this failure?

- How does the woman's act of anointing Jesus successfully imagine the world Jesus proclaims and creates?

- What role does imagination play in works of charity? In works of justice? Does one require more imagination than the other, and how so?

CLOSING YOUR SESSION

Read aloud from *Context*: "If we are willing to do the difficult work, if we will collaborate with the Spirit who is always leading us toward justice, then we can transform the world into a place in which everyone has enough." Lead a discussion of what Josh calls "the difficult questions" Jesus's message evokes, encouraging participants to answer as specifically as possible in the contexts of their own lives, their community, and/or your congregation and be ready and willing to model such specific answers yourself:

- How will we use our resources individually and collectively?

- Are we willing to be inconvenienced personally to see real change societally?

- Do we believe the world can become a just and equitable place?

On the newsprint or markerboard, write specific ideas for making change real that arise from your group's discussion. Together, make a plan for holding yourselves accountable for taking the next concrete step toward at least one of these changes (for example: contacting an elected official, raising an issue with your church's council, becoming a volunteer with a community organization pursuing a just goal).

CLOSING PRAYER

God, ignite our imaginations, that we may commit ourselves to the difficult work of justice. Empower us to challenge the systems and powers that keep this world from becoming more like the world of which you dream, the world in which all your children have enough. Amen.

SESSION 4

"For Surely I Know the Plans I Have for You"
(Jeremiah 29:11)

SESSION OBJECTIVES

This session will help participants:

+ Reflect on how they have heard Jeremiah 29:11 interpreted in their past.

+ Understand, in broad outline, the historical background of Jeremiah's letter to exiled Judeans in Babylon.

+ Examine Jeremiah's critiques of those who worshipped in the Temple in Jerusalem prior to the Babylonian Exile and ponder those critiques' continuing relevance.

+ Consider the purpose of Jeremiah's letter to the exilic community in Babylon, and reconsider 29:11 in that original context.

+ Articulate new applications of Jeremiah 29:11 for their own and others' lives.

BIBLICAL FOUNDATIONS

The word that came to Jeremiah from the Lord: *Stand in the gate of the* Lord's *house, and proclaim there this word, and say, Hear the word of the* Lord, *all you people of Judah, you who enter these gates to worship the* Lord. *Thus says the* Lord *of hosts, the God of Israel: Amend your ways and your doings, and let me dwell with you in this place. Do not trust in these deceptive words: "This is the temple of the* Lord, *the temple of the* Lord, *the temple of the* Lord."

For if you truly amend your ways and your doings, if you truly act justly one with another, if you do not oppress the alien, the orphan, and the widow or shed innocent blood in this place, and if you do not go after other gods to your own hurt, then I will dwell with you in this place, in the land that I gave to your ancestors forever and ever.

(Jeremiah 7:1-7)

These are the words of the letter that the prophet Jeremiah sent from Jerusalem to the remaining elders among the exiles and to the priests, the prophets, and all the people whom Nebuchadnezzar had taken into exile from Jerusalem to Babylon. This was after King Jeconiah and the queen mother, the court officials, the leaders of Judah and Jerusalem, the artisans, and the smiths had departed from Jerusalem. The letter was sent by the hand of Elasah son of Shaphan and Gemariah son of Hilkiah, whom King Zedekiah of Judah sent to Babylon to King Nebuchadnezzar of Babylon. It said: Thus says the Lord *of hosts, the God of Israel, to all the exiles whom I have sent into exile from Jerusalem to Babylon: Build houses and live in them; plant gardens and eat what they produce. Take wives and have sons and daughters; take wives for your sons, and give your daughters in marriage, that they may bear sons and daughters; multiply there, and do not decrease. But seek the welfare of the city where I have sent you into exile, and pray to the* Lord *on its behalf, for in its welfare you will find your welfare. For thus says the* Lord *of hosts, the God of Israel: Do not let the prophets and the diviners who are among you deceive you, and do not listen to your dreams that you dream, for it is a lie that they are prophesying to you in my name; I did not send them, says the* Lord.

For thus says the LORD: Only when Babylon's seventy years are completed will I visit you, and I will fulfill to you my promise and bring you back to this place. For surely I know the plans I have for you, says the LORD, plans for your welfare and not for harm, to give you a future with hope. Then when you call upon me and come and pray to me, I will hear you. When you search for me, you will find me; if you seek me with all your heart, I will let you find me, says the LORD, and I will restore your fortunes and gather you from all the nations and all the places where I have driven you, says the LORD, and I will bring you back to the place from which I sent you into exile.

(*Jeremiah 29:1-14*)

BEFORE YOUR SESSION

+ Carefully and prayerfully read the Biblical Foundations several times. Consult a trusted study Bible and/or commentaries for additional background information.

+ Carefully read *Context: Putting Scripture in Its Place*, chapter 4. Note topics about which you have questions or want to research further before your session.

+ You will need: Bibles for in-person participants and/or screen slides prepared with Scripture texts for sharing (note the translation you use); newsprint or a markerboard and markers (for in-person sessions).

+ If using the DVD or streaming video, preview the session 4 video segment. Choose the best time in your session plan for viewing it.

STARTING YOUR SESSION

Welcome participants. Read aloud Jeremiah 29:11. Discuss:

+ How many of you are familiar with this Bible verse?

+ If you are familiar with this verse, when have you encountered it?

- What interpretation(s) of this verse have you heard that you've found meaningful? Have you heard any interpretation(s) of it you found less meaningful? Why?
- In *Context*, Josh writes that, as a youth, he heard this verse interpreted to mean God had a specific plan for his life. Have you ever been told, or told yourself, "God has a plan for your life?" How do you react to that claim?

Tell participants this session will explore what Jeremiah 29:11 meant in its original context, and whether it supports the idea that God has a plan for our lives.

OPENING PRAYER

God, we trust that you are with us always, in both the good and bad, the joy and the sadness. Open our hearts and minds to see the wisdom, challenge, and invitation of Jeremiah's words. May we be encouraged and stretched by what we learn. Amen.

WATCH SESSION VIDEO

Watch the session 4 video segment together. Discuss:

- What did Josh say in this video that most interested, intrigued, surprised, or confused you? Why?
- What questions does this video raise for you?

BOOK DISCUSSION QUESTIONS

Marching Toward Exile

Read aloud from *Context* or summarize the history of Assyria's defeat of the Northern Kingdom of Israel in 721 BCE, and of Assyria's threat to

Judah two decades later. You may wish to read aloud or refer participants to Isaiah 37:15-20, 33-35 as part of your summary; these verses are excerpts from King Hezekiah's prayer, which Josh mentions, and Isaiah's assurance that Assyria will not conquer Jerusalem. Tell participants that by Jeremiah's time, a century later, a belief in Jerusalem's inviolability had emerged (see, for example, Psalm 48).

Recruit a volunteer to read aloud Jeremiah 7:1-7 (or through verse 15). Discuss:

+ Where does God instruct Jeremiah to preach this sermon (verses 1-2)? Why is this setting significant?

+ Why does Jeremiah say calling the Temple "the temple of the LORD" is "deceptive" (verse 4)?

+ What is preventing God from dwelling with God's people in the Temple, as God wanted to do (verses 5-7)?

+ Why does Jeremiah's sermon invoke the memory of Shiloh, God's sanctuary in the Northern Kingdom ("the offspring of Ephraim") (verses 12-15)?

+ According to Jeremiah's sermon, how is the people's memory of the past leading them to draw the wrong conclusions about their present? When have you seen communities of faith, including your own, learn the wrong lessons from their past?

+ How can and does religious faith become a license for unfaithful behavior today, as Jeremiah's sermon indicts his nation's faith in his day?

+ Jeremiah preached against injustice and idolatry in his nation. What forms, if any, do you think these sins take in your nation today? How do you and your congregation respond to them?

+ Why did Jeremiah urge his nation to submit to, rather than resist, King Nebuchadnezzar and the Babylonians? Why did

King Jehoiakim of Judah choose to resist instead? Whose choice do you think seemed more reasonable and responsible at the time, and why?

+ Babylon's siege of Jerusalem and deportation of its leading citizens in 597 BCE and its destruction of the city a decade later bore out Jeremiah's call for submission. Can God's people only determine the validity of a prophetic message in retrospect? If so, why does God send prophets? If not, how else can God's people discern a trustworthy prophetic message?

The Promise to the Exilic Community

Recruit a volunteer to read aloud Jeremiah 29:1-14 (or through verse 23). Discuss:

+ Josh says the prophetic task is twofold: to warn and disturb, and to give comfort and hope. How does Jeremiah's letters to those deported from Jerusalem in 597 BCE do both? Which aspect of Jeremiah's task, if either, do you think is dominant in the letter, and why?

+ What is the "bad news/good news assessment" of the exiles' situation Jeremiah's letter offers? How do you imagine the exiles responded to this assessment, especially its call to "seek the welfare" of their place of exile (verse 7)?

+ How does Jeremiah's letter challenge the ancient world's common belief that gods were connected, or even confined, to the places in which people worshipped them?

+ Josh says the word usually translated "plans" in verse 11 is better translated "thoughts" or "intentions." Why?

+ "The idea that God plans everything, every detail of our lives, is problematic." Do you agree? Why or why not? How do some believers find the idea "comforting" while others find it "unnerving"? What, if anything, could these two perspectives learn from each other?

+ God's intentions toward the exilic community are for, in the original Hebrew, *shalom*. How is *shalom* best defined, according to Josh? Which aspects of his definition most resonate with you, and why? What words or images might you choose to convey the rich meaning of *shalom*?

+ Does the Creation story in Genesis 2–3 help you understand God's intentions for *shalom*, as Josh suggests it does? Why or why not?

+ Josh says the phrase in Jeremiah 29:11 usually translated "a future with hope" is more literally translated "an expected end." How, if at all, does this more literal translation change how you understand the verse? Do you find it more comforting, less comforting, or about as comforting as the more usual translation? Why?

Applying Jeremiah 29:11 Today

+ Josh cautions against appropriating "the comfort and hope being offered to an oppressed group of people" when interpreting Jeremiah 29:11 today. Beyond studying the text's original context, what else can comfortable and privileged Christians do to read and understand this verse from a perspective closer to that of its original audience?

+ Josh urges readers to remember Jeremiah wrote his letter to a community. How well or poorly do you think our society balances individual and communal identity? Why? How does remembering Jeremiah wrote his letter to a community change the way we understand it?

+ "Flourishing doesn't just happen," writes Josh, but "must be intentionally cultivated." What practical examples of intentionally cultivating flourishing, or *shalom*, can you offer?
+ How does your congregation take intentional, practical steps to cultivate its own flourishing? What about the flourishing of the community beyond itself?
+ How should "sensitivity to the complexity of human life and experience" shape the ways in which we interpret Jeremiah 29:11, especially for other people? Has the suggestion that something did or did not happen according to "God's plan" ever upset or harmed you? How readily do you talk about "God's plan" with respect to what does or doesn't happen to and for other people, and why?
+ Josh says sometimes all we can do is sit "in the mystery and pain" of human life, "knowing that it all matters and it's all holy." Have you ever had such an experience? How, if at all, did it shape what you believe about "God's plan"?

CLOSING YOUR SESSION

In *Context*, Josh suggests God has hopes and intentions for us "that we would be shaped and formed in and by love" but doesn't control the outcome, leaving us free, in love, "to return or resist that love." Discuss:

+ How do you react to Josh's understanding of God's "plans" for humanity?
+ How does God's refusal to force God's intentions on us preserve and respect human freedom? How does human freedom give meaning to the ways we enact God's intentions?

+ "God dreams of a world where all of us flourish," writes Josh, "where we all find the healing and wholeness that were meant to be ours." Do you think God's dream is solely dependent upon human participation to become reality? Why or why not?

+ What is one specific way you can and will "partner with God" before the next session to make God's intentions real, as an individual or with your congregation?

CLOSING PRAYER

God, we know your intentions toward us are good. You will the flourishing of all your children. May we be active participants with you in making that vision a reality. Amen.

[handwritten: Paul also wrote Ephesians, Colossians, Philemon, while incarcerated]

SESSION 5

[handwritten: did not write in a moment of crisis]

[handwritten: Paul & Timothy]

"I Can Do All Things Through Him Who Strengthens Me"

(Philippians 4:13)

SESSION OBJECTIVES

This session will help participants:

+ Assess the common "motivational" interpretation of Philippians 4:13.

+ Appreciate the tone of gratitude and love that characterizes Paul's letter to the Philippians.

+ Understand how the Philippian congregation provided for Paul's needs during his imprisonment.

+ Consider Philippians 4:13 as a statement about how Christ can transform our experience of weakness and suffering, rather than necessarily save us from them.

- Write messages of gratitude to friends who have embodied Christ's strength and encouragement for them.

BIBLICAL FOUNDATIONS

Paul and Timothy, servants of Christ Jesus,

To all the saints in Christ Jesus who are in Philippi, with the bishops and deacons:

Grace to you and peace from God our Father and the Lord Jesus Christ.

I thank my God for every remembrance of you, always in every one of my prayers for all of you, praying with joy for your partnership in the gospel from the first day until now. I am confident of this, that the one who began a good work in you will continue to complete it until the day of Jesus Christ. It is right for me to think this way about all of you, because I hold you in my heart, for all of you are my partners in God's grace, both in my imprisonment and in the defense and confirmation of the gospel. For God is my witness, how I long for all of you with the tender affection of Christ Jesus. And this is my prayer, that your love may overflow more and more with knowledge and full insight to help you to determine what really matters, so that in the day of Christ you may be pure and blameless, having produced the harvest of righteousness that comes through Jesus Christ for the glory and praise of God.

(Philippians 1:1-11)

I rejoice in the Lord greatly that now at last you have revived your concern for me; indeed, you were concerned for me but had no opportunity to show it. Not that I am referring to being in need, for I have learned to be content with whatever I have. I know what it is to have little, and I know what it is to have plenty. In any and all circumstances I have learned the secret of being well-fed and of going hungry, of having plenty and of being in need. I can do all things through him who strengthens me. In any case, it was kind of you to share my distress.

(Philippians 4:10-14)

BEFORE YOUR SESSION

+ Carefully and prayerfully read the Biblical Foundations several times. Consult a trusted study Bible and/or commentaries for additional background information.

+ Carefully read *Context: Putting Scripture in Its Place*, chapter 5. Note topics about which you have questions or want to research further before your session.

+ You will need: Bibles for in-person participants and/or screen slides prepared with Scripture texts for sharing (note the translation you use); newsprint or a markerboard and markers (for in-person sessions); scrap paper.

+ If using the DVD or streaming video, preview the session 5 video segment. Choose the best time in your session plan for viewing it.

+ *Optional*: Gather or print out a number of inspirational and motivational posters, including any you may find that use Philippians 4:13; a blank thank-you note for each participant.

STARTING YOUR SESSION

Welcome participants. Ask volunteers to describe the most memorable motivational poster they have seen—whether because it was particularly effective, laughably ineffective, exceptionally funny, or any other reason. If you have gathered a selection of motivational posters, show them to the group and ask them to discuss which one(s) they like and dislike most, and why.

Summarize Josh's observation that Philippians 4:13 is a verse often used for motivational purposes. Ask participants if they have ever encountered it as a motivational text or have found it motivational themselves. Ask participants what other Bible verses, if any, they consider motivational.

Read aloud from *Context:* "I don't think it's wrong or out of place to search for consolation or relief in the words of Scripture....At the same time, I do firmly believe it's important to know a bit about the context in and from which these passages come to us." Tell participants this session will help your group understand Philippians 4:13 in context, to best determine how motivational it can be.

OPENING PRAYER

God, help us hear these ancient words in a fresh way. Challenge our preconceived ideas and help us be open to what we might learn together. Amen.

WATCH SESSION VIDEO

Watch the session 5 video segment together. Discuss:

+ What did Josh say in this video that most interested, intrigued, surprised, or confused you? Why?
+ What questions does this video raise for you?

BOOK DISCUSSION QUESTIONS

A Letter of Love

Recruit a volunteer to read aloud Philippians 1:1-11. Discuss:

+ How would you describe the tone with which Paul addresses the Philippians in these verses?
+ For what specific reasons does Paul give God thanks for the Philippians? What is Paul's prayer for them?
+ Review Josh's account of Philippi's history and significance. Why was Philippi's status as a colony of Rome significant?

How does this status inform Paul's reminder to his letter's recipients that they are citizens of heaven (see 3:20)?

+ Skim the account in Acts 16:11-40 of Paul and Silas's ministry in Philippi. How might these incidents have helped forge the "deep connection" between Paul and the Philippians of which Josh writes?

+ We have no way of knowing why Euodia and Syntyche were at odds, but what does Paul say about his concern for them (4:2-3)? What insights does Paul's approach to these women's conflict offer Christians in conflict with each other today?

A Letter from Prison

+ Why does Paul regard his imprisonment with joy (1:12-14)? Why does he regard what may be his impending death the same way (1:18b-26)?

+ What are the most difficult circumstances, if any, in which you have experienced joy? Do you agree that "making space for joy" in hardship is "a necessity," as Josh states Paul does? Why or why not? If so, how can we do so? If not, what attitude(s) toward difficult circumstances ought Christians adopt?

+ "In the Roman era, prisoners would have been dependent on family and friends to supply their needs for food, water, and clothing while in prison." In what difficult circumstances have you supplied these needs for someone else out of concern for them? Has anyone ever supplied them for you in hardship?

+ Josh points out the Philippians "sprang into action" when they learned of Paul's imprisonment. What difficult circumstances others face cause your congregation to spring into action, and what forms does that action take?

+ The Philippians sent Epaphroditus to Paul with their provisions for him. What happened to him after he reached Paul (2:25-30)? Who do you know or know of who has risked personal safety to minister to others' needs? What is the biggest risk you have taken for "the work of Christ" (verse 30)?

+ How is your congregation involved in ministry to those who are imprisoned, or how could it be?

+ Josh discusses how the Philippian congregation contributed to the needs of believers in Jerusalem more readily and more generously than other, more affluent congregations, such as the one in Corinth. When have you witnessed a similar pattern of seemingly contradictory generosity? What do you think accounts for it?

Putting Philippians 4:13 in Context

Recruit a volunteer to read aloud Philippians 4:10-13. Discuss:

+ How would you explain, in your own words, the main point Paul is making in these verses?

+ Josh explains the word translated "secret" (verse 12) refers to an insight that comes only through connection to God. Have you ever experienced this kind of insight? How can we tell when such insight actually comes from God?

+ Josh's literal, unpolished translation of verse 13 is, "All things I am strong for in the one strengthening me." How is this claim like and/or unlike the common "motivational" interpretation of verse 13, that Christ always allows us to overcome challenges?

+ Josh says Paul's words reflect the reality of human living: "So often joy and grief are not mutually exclusive experiences, but simultaneous ones." When and how, if ever, have joy and grief been simultaneous experiences for you?

+ How did the story of Jesus "reframe" weakness for Paul? Why did Jesus not avoid weakness and suffering for himself? Why does he not always save others from suffering and weakness?

+ In Paul's world, Josh states, "weakness was seen as something to be masked." How does our world expect people to mask weakness?

+ To what extent is your congregation a space in which people can safely reveal their weakness? How do you help each other keep going in your weaknesses?

+ Josh thinks the biggest problem with the common "motivational" understanding of Philippians 4:13 is that it gives people an unrealistic view of human life and Christian faith, much as his family's "Genie Pass" gave them an unrealistic view of a trip to Walt Disney World. Do you think the "motivational" use of this verse is as potentially harmful as Josh thinks it is? Why or why not?

+ Have you ever been made to feel worse about failure because others told you that you were to blame? How were you or have you been able to challenge this assumption?

+ Josh states that the promise of Philippians 4:13 "has always been strength and empowerment, even in moments of loss, grief, and failure." When, if ever, have you experienced this promise as a truth in your life? What about witnessing it as true in the lives of others?

CLOSING YOUR SESSION

Josh writes that "Paul knew Jesus as a source of empowerment and strength" not only internally and emotionally but also through "Paul's communities, friends, and partners in his work." Speaking for himself, Josh writes, "Every time I have met God in any tangible way, God was always wearing human skin."

Distribute scrap paper (or, if you have them, a blank thank-you note to each participant). Remind participants that Paul wrote Philippians not to be the inspired Scripture the church ultimately recognized it to be, but as a message "drenched in affection, gratitude, and joy" to friends who had embodied Christ's encouragement and strength for him. Invite participants to spend a few minutes drafting such a note to someone who has done the same for them. Tell them they do not necessarily have to send what they write in this moment and can use this opportunity to write a "first draft," but encourage them to think of someone to whom they would want to send such a letter, and to make some specific notes about why. After allowing participants time to think and write, invite volunteers to briefly talk about the note they would send or to read what they have written aloud.

CLOSING PRAYER

God, we know that life will inevitably bring challenges, difficulties, and grief. Give us strength and courage for those moments. We live hopefully, knowing that life will also bring joy and happiness. Help us embrace and be encouraged by those times as well. Amen.

SESSION 6

Sodom and Gomorrah

(Genesis 19)

SESSION OBJECTIVES

This session will help participants:

+ Name and confront examples of prejudice and hatred directed against members of the LGTBQ+ community, including examples of such prejudice and hatred from Christians.
+ Appreciate the importance of *xenia* (hospitality toward strangers) as a virtue in the ancient world and compare and contrast hospitality's importance in their own society.
+ Closely read the story of Sodom as a story about an extreme failure to provide hospitality to strangers.
+ Consider additional biblical testimony about the guilt of Sodom.
+ Think and talk together about ways their congregation can more faithfully extend hospitality to all people, especially those who are most marginalized and vulnerable.

BIBLICAL FOUNDATIONS

The two angels came to Sodom in the evening, and Lot was sitting in the gateway of Sodom. When Lot saw them, he rose to meet them and bowed down with his face to the ground. He said, "Please, my lords, turn aside to your servant's house and spend the night and wash your feet; then you can rise early and go on your way." They said, "No; we will spend the night in the square." But he urged them strongly, so they turned aside to him and entered his house, and he made them a feast and baked unleavened bread, and they ate. But before they lay down, the men of the city, the men of Sodom, both young and old, all the people to the last man, surrounded the house, and they called to Lot, "Where are the men who came to you tonight? Bring them out to us, so that we may know them." Lot went out of the door to the men, shut the door after him, and said, "I beg you, my brothers, do not act so wickedly. Look, I have two daughters who have not known a man; let me bring them out to you, and do to them as you please; only do nothing to these men, for they have come under the shelter of my roof." But they replied, "Stand back!" And they said, "This fellow came here as an alien, and he would play the judge! Now we will deal worse with you than with them." Then they pressed hard against the man Lot and came near the door to break it down. But the men inside reached out their hands and brought Lot into the house with them and shut the door. And they struck with blindness the men who were at the door of the house, both small and great, so that they were unable to find the door.

Then the men said to Lot, "Have you anyone else here? Sons-in-law, sons, daughters, or anyone you have in the city—bring them out of the place. For we are about to destroy this place, because the outcry against its people has become great before the LORD, and the LORD has sent us to destroy it." So Lot went out and said to his sons-in-law, who were to marry his daughters, "Up, get out of this place, for the LORD is about to destroy the city." But he seemed to his sons-in-law to be jesting.

When morning dawned, the angels urged Lot, saying, "Get up, take your wife and your two daughters who are here, or else you will be consumed in the punishment of the city." But he lingered, so the men seized him and his wife and his two daughters by the hand, the LORD being merciful to him, and they brought him out and left him outside the city. When they had brought them outside, they said, "Flee for your life; do not look back or stop anywhere in the plain; flee to the hills, or else you will be consumed." And Lot said to them, "Oh, no, my lords; your servant has found favor with you, and you have shown me great kindness in saving my life, but I cannot flee to the hills, for fear the disaster will overtake me and I die. Look, that city is near enough to flee to, and it is a little one. Let me escape there—is it not a little one?—and my life will be saved!" He said to him, "Very well, I grant you this favor too and will not overthrow the city of which you have spoken. Hurry, escape there, for I can do nothing until you arrive there." Therefore the city was called Zoar. The sun had risen on the earth when Lot came to Zoar.

Then the LORD rained on Sodom and Gomorrah sulfur and fire from the LORD out of heaven, and he overthrew those cities and all the plain and all the inhabitants of the cities and what grew on the ground. But Lot's wife, behind him, looked back, and she became a pillar of salt.

Abraham went early in the morning to the place where he had stood before the LORD, and he looked down toward Sodom and Gomorrah and toward all the land of the plain and saw the smoke of the land going up like the smoke of a furnace.

So it was that, when God destroyed the cities of the plain, God remembered Abraham and sent Lot out of the midst of the overthrow, when he overthrew the cities in which Lot had settled.

(Genesis 19:1-29)

BEFORE YOUR SESSION

+ Carefully and prayerfully read the Biblical Foundations several times. Consult a trusted study Bible and/or commentaries for additional background information.

+ Carefully read *Context: Putting Scripture in Its Place*, chapter 6. Note topics about which you have questions or want to research further before your session.

+ You will need: Bibles for in-person participants and/or screen slides prepared with Scripture texts for sharing (note the translation you use); newsprint or a markerboard and markers (for in-person sessions)

+ If using the DVD or streaming video, preview the session 6 video segment. Choose the best time in your session plan for viewing it.

STARTING YOUR SESSION

Welcome participants. Because this is your last session, invite volunteers to share the most interesting, surprising, confusing, or frustrating thing they have learned during the group's study so far. Start discussion by offering your own response first. Thank them for their participation in this study.

Tell participants Josh thinks this session's Scripture, the story of Sodom and Gomorrah, is the most difficult of the stories you have studied to read in its original context, but also "the most important."

Ask:

+ What do you think of when you hear the phrase "Sodom and Gomorrah"?

+ Have you heard this story used to condemn the LGBTQ+ community?

+ How have you witnessed and/or experienced prejudice and hatred directed against members of the LGBTQ+ community? When has such prejudice and hatred come from Christians?

Read aloud from *Context*: "[T]his story...is the most extreme example of how failure to understand the context of the Bible can lead to real

harm being done to real people....Sadly, this is a text with a body count."
Tell participants this session will help your group reevaluate "the sin of
Sodom" against which Scripture testifies.

OPENING PRAYER

*God, you call us to love, not hate. Guide our study of a difficult story in
Scripture, lead us to new insight and keep us always from abusing it as a
weapon. Amen.*

WATCH SESSION VIDEO

Watch the session 6 video segment together. Discuss:

+ What did Josh say in this video that most interested, intrigued,
  surprised, or confused you? Why?
+ What questions does this video raise for you?

BOOK DISCUSSION QUESTIONS

A City with a Bad Reputation

+ When have you, like Lot, found yourself "in the wrong place at
  the wrong time"? Did you end up then and there by your own
  doing, as Lot did, or through other circumstances?
+ Josh points out negative associations with "the east" and
  eastward movement in Genesis. How do you find these
  associations at work in these texts: Genesis 3:22-24; 4:13-16;
  11:1-4; 13:8-13?
+ Read Genesis 18:16-21. What motivates God to go and
  investigate Sodom and Gomorrah? What does God intend to
  do about the cities, and why does God decide to tell Abraham?

+ Read Genesis 18:22-33. How does Abraham intercede for the cities? Why? When and why, if ever, have you felt like holding God to God's own standards of righteousness, as Abraham did? How did this desire shape your prayer and action?

+ Are there places you avoid or to which you would never go because they have a bad reputation? How do God's resolve to see Sodom and Gomorrah and Abraham's ability to imagine righteous people in these cities each challenge our tendency to believe the worst of what we have been told about someplace or someone?

Understanding the Ancient World

+ Read or review Josh's summary of the story of Baucis and Philemon from Ovid's *Metamorphoses* (8 CE). How does this story demonstrate the importance of the ancient ideal of *xenia*? Why was showing hospitality to strangers one of the ancient world's cardinal virtues?

+ Read Genesis 18:1-15. How do Abraham and Sarah demonstrate *xenia* in this story? How is their hospitality rewarded?

+ Why does the author of Hebrews tell early Christians to show hospitality to strangers (13:2)? How does this instruction reflect the importance of *xenia*?

+ When have you been the recipient of hospitality as a stranger? When have you shown hospitality to strangers? Was your hospitality rewarded and, if so, how?

+ Should those who show hospitality to strangers expect a reward? Why or why not?

+ How important a virtue in your community is *xenia*? How important a virtue do you think it is in your society as a whole? Explain your answers.

+ How does or how could your congregation encourage the virtue of hospitality to strangers in today's world?

The Real Sin of Sodom

Recruit volunteers to read aloud Genesis 19:1-29, taking these roles: the narrator, Lot, the two angels, and a representative man or several men of Sodom. Discuss:

+ How does Lot extend hospitality to the two angels? How is his hospitality rewarded?

+ How do the men of Sodom want to treat the angels? Why does the narrator stress the size of the crowd surrounding Lot's home (verse 4)?

+ How does Lot's offer of his virgin daughters to the crowd affect your opinion of him? How do you imagine Lot's daughters, their betrothed husbands, and his wife felt about Lot's offer? What might Lot's offer suggest about the corrosive influence of sin in Sodom?

+ What do the men of Sodom mean by accusing Lot of wanting to "play the judge" (verse 9)? What does their remark reveal about their attitude toward strangers?

+ What does the men of Sodom's violence reveal about them?

+ Why do you think Lot's sons-in-law believe he is "jesting" (verse 14)? Have you ever failed to take a threat to your safety and well-being seriously enough? What happened?

+ Why do the angels command Lot to not look back as he and his family leave (verse 17)? Why do you imagine Lot's wife does (verse 26)?

+ "This is not a story about consensual same-sex relationships," writes Josh, but "about hostility and hate toward the outsider." Do you find Josh's argument convincing? Why or why not?

+ "What we see in Sodom is not an issue of a few individuals engaging in hostility, but a societal problem." Where do you find the problem of xenophobia (the fear of strangers) in your society? How does your culture "abuse and traumatize" the outsiders in its midst?

Calling in Backup

Form three small teams of participants. Assign one of the following Scriptures to each team:

+ Isaiah 1:10-17
+ Ezekiel 16:48-50
+ Matthew 10:9-15

Ask each team to discuss what its assigned passage says, directly or indirectly, about the sin of Sodom. After allowing sufficient time for reading and discussion, bring the whole group together. Invite a volunteer from each team to summarize their team's discussion.

Use these questions as needed to bring out important points from team discussions:

+ Although Isaiah was preaching to the kingdom of Judah in the eighth century BCE, he associates it with Sodom because he sees it committing similar sins. What are the sins for which God, through Isaiah, calls God's people to account? How does the prophet call on the people to change?

+ According to Josh, the Hebrew word for "abomination" means something that is "ritually or ethically impure" for God's people, and not necessarily a "sin" in and of itself. Of what "abominations" does God accuse God's people through Ezekiel? Would you consider these "abominations" sinful?

Why or why not? How do you see these same "abominations" in
society today?

+ To what extent does Jesus's invocation of Sodom and Gomorrah
in Matthew 10:15 reinforce the idea that these cities' sins had
to do with a lack of hospitality to strangers, considering his
instructions to his disciples in the preceding verses?

CLOSING YOUR SESSION

Read aloud from *Context*:

"The sin of Sodom was not ... being Queer. The sin of Sodom was being
hostile and inhospitable.... As [Christians] have tried to avoid the sin
of Sodom by excluding the LGTBQ+ community, we have actually
committed that very sin.... Of course, this story's impact stretches even
further, calling us as people of faith to the practice of hospitality toward
all of God's children."

Discuss:

+ How does your congregation extend hospitality to members of
the LGTBQ+ community? To what extent does it encourage
these individuals' full participation in the community's
life? What more, if anything, would you like to see your
congregation doing to welcome and include them?

+ Josh argues "budgets are moral documents." How well does your
congregation's budget prioritize justice for those who are poor,
marginalized, and strangers in society? What about your own
personal budget?

+ How, if at all, does your church work to be hospitable to
immigrants? What more could your congregation be doing?

- How does your congregation practice hospitality toward people of other faith traditions, or of no faith tradition?

CLOSING PRAYER

God, yours is a generous and expansive welcome. May your Spirit strengthen us to build larger tables instead of taller fences, that our community may more fully reflect the wideness of your love and the wide embrace of your arms, including the whole world. Amen.

Read the Bible for the First Time— Again.

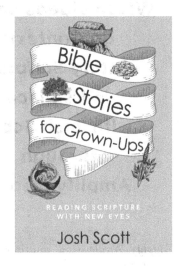

In *Bible Stories for Grown-Ups: Reading Scripture with New Eyes*, pastor Josh Scott looks at familiar Bible stories and reveals new details and interpretations for an adult audience. This six-week Bible study considers stories many read as children including Noah's Ark, the binding of Isaac, Jonah and the big fish, Jesus and Zacchaeus, Jesus healing a blind man, and the parable of the talents. Scott reimagines these stories and opens new visions for readers to understand well-known pieces of Scripture in our current cultural environment.

The book can be read alone or used by small groups and can be used anytime throughout the year. Additional components include video teaching sessions featuring Josh Scott, and a comprehensive leader guide, making this perfect as a six-week group study done throughout the year.

ISBN 978-1-7910-2662-2

*Also available Leader Guide (ISBN 978-1-7910-2664-6)
and DVD (ISBN 978-1-7910-2666-0)*

Available wherever fine books are sold.

Watch videos based on *Context: Putting Scripture in Its Place* with Josh Scott through Amplify Media.

Amplify Media is a multimedia platform that delivers high quality, searchable content with an emphasis on Wesleyan perspectives for churchwide, group, or individual use on any device at any time. In a world of sometimes overwhelming choices, Amplify gives church leaders and congregants media capabilities that are contemporary, relevant, effective and, most importantly, affordable and sustainable.

With *Amplify Media* church leaders can:

+ Provide a reliable source of Christian content through a Wesleyan lens for teaching, training, and inspiration in a customizable library
+ Deliver their own preaching and worship content in a way the congregation knows and appreciates
+ Build the church's capacity to innovate with engaging content and accessible technology
+ Equip the congregation to better understand the Bible and its application
+ Deepen discipleship beyond the church walls

Ask your group leader or pastor about Amplify Media and sign up today at www.AmplifyMedia.com.

Printed in the USA
CPSIA information can be obtained
at www.ICGtesting.com
LVHW031739120924
790588LV00006B/25